A MAN'S MANUAL

EVERYTHING I FACED WHILE MY WIFE WAS PREGNANT

PRANEEV DEOJA CHETTRI

Made with ♥ on the Notion Press Platform
www.notionpress.com

To all the unknown men,
standing quietly beside their pregnant wives,
navigating a journey no one taught them how to walk.

To the husbands who held back tears,
swallowed fear,
and showed up every single day —
even when they didn't have the answers.

This book is for you.
For the sleepless nights, the whispered reassurances,
the awkward doctor visits, and the uncertain moments you made brave.

May you find strength in these pages,
wisdom in these stories,
and the comfort of knowing —
you are not alone.

And to Yudenla Lama,
for being the inspiration behind every word.

Contents

Preface

When my wife whispered, "I think I'm pregnant," my world didn't just change — it cracked open.

I wasn't ready for the storm of emotions that followed. The joy, the fear, the late-night Googling, the second-guessing, the whispered arguments, the random tears, the cravings, the hormonal rollercoasters, the doctor visits, and the silence — oh, the silence, when you don't know what to say, but you know she needs you to say something.

This book isn't a medical guide. It's not a clinical breakdown of pregnancy trimesters. It's not a list of dos and don'ts from an expert. This is a raw, unfiltered, brutally honest story of one man trying to show up for the woman he loves during the most vulnerable and powerful time of her life.

I wrote this book because I couldn't find anything like it when I needed it most. There were guides for moms, apps for symptoms, and forums for baby names. But there was nothing that told me — the man, the husband, the soon-to-be father — what I should feel, say, or do.

How do you comfort your wife when she cries for no reason?

What do you say when she asks, "Will you still find me attractive when I'm big?"

How do you remain calm when her platelets drop in the final weeks?

What do you do when you feel terrified but can't show it?

These are the questions this book explores — not with textbook answers, but with stories. Real ones. From the first pregnancy test to the operating room where I heard our daughter cry for the first time.

And here's the thing: by the end of it all, I learned something I wish every man knew before he stepped into fatherhood.

I won't spoil it here.

But if you read this — every page, every lesson, every confession — you'll know.

You'll feel it.

And you'll be better for it.

Let this book be your manual — not because I did everything perfectly, but because I didn't. And still, I became the man my wife needed... and the father my daughter deserves.

Now turn the page.

Let's walk this journey together.

— Praneev Deoja Chettri

Acknowledgements

Behind every strong man is a circle of quiet, powerful support — people who held the flashlight when I couldn't see the way. This book wouldn't exist without them.

First and foremost, I want to thank my wife, Yudenla Lama — the heart of this journey, the quiet strength behind every chapter, and the reason I found parts of myself I didn't know existed. Your grace, patience, and resilience during every stage of this pregnancy taught me what true courage looks like. You gave life — not just to our daughter, but to a deeper version of me.

To my sisters Pratistha Deoja Lama and Shradha Bhandari, thank you for being my sounding boards — for helping me understand the emotional storms Yudenla was weathering, and for always guiding me with empathy when I didn't know what the "right" thing to do was. Your advice was like a compass in moments I felt lost.

To my elder brother Pravesh Deoja, thank you for constantly checking in, for making sure I never felt alone, and for always reminding me that no matter where we are, family stands close.

To my mother — you have this beautiful way of walking into a room and lighting it up. Thank you for being a constant source of positivity and warmth, for brightening our days, and for grounding us with your presence.

To my mother-in-law — your help around the house, your care, and your quiet strength kept both Yudenla and me sane when things got overwhelming. Thank you for stepping in so selflessly and being there when we needed it most.

To my boss, Vikas Verma — thank you for your patience and unwavering support. At a time when work and life collided in the most intense ways, your understanding made space for me to focus on what mattered.

To Dr. Nevidita Jha and the entire team at Sparsh Hospital — thank you for being more than just doctors and nurses. Thank you for being our support system 24/7, for answering every late-night worry, and for ensuring that both my wife and daughter came out of this journey safe, healthy, and whole.

This book is not just mine — it belongs to everyone who stood beside us, held our hands, sent us strength, and showed us love. I simply wrote the words. You all made the story possible.

With all my heart,

Prologue

They say when a woman gets pregnant, a mother is born. But what no one talks about — what almost never makes it into the books or conversations — is that a father is quietly being born too.

I wasn't prepared. Not for the hormonal waves, not for the mood swings, not for the late-night cravings, the fear of scans, or the endless advice that poured in from every corner. I wasn't prepared to see my wife in pain and feel so helpless. I wasn't ready to feel joy and fear in the same breath.

This book is not about perfect parenting or expert advice. It's not even about fatherhood in the traditional sense.

This book is about becoming. About what happens to a man when he stands beside a woman who's growing a new life inside her — and what it demands of him emotionally, mentally, and spiritually.

It's about what I learned when my wife didn't smile for days, when her tears didn't have reasons, when her body changed faster than I could comprehend. It's about what I realized when I wanted to walk away from the frustration but chose to stay and listen instead. It's about how my role wasn't to fix anything — it was to feel everything with her.

This journey stripped me down and rebuilt me — into a softer, stronger, more aware version of myself.

This is not a manual for men who want to be perfect.

This is for the men who are trying. For the ones holding their partner's hand through ultrasounds, googling "what does a contraction feel like?" at 2 AM, and trying to keep it together when everything feels like it's falling apart.

If you're one of those men — or even if you're just curious about what it means to stand tall in the chaos of pregnancy beside someone you love — this book is for you.

Let's walk through it together.

CHAPTER I

The Unexpected News

It was August 31, 2024. A day that began like any other but ended up changing the course of my life forever. I was behind the wheel, cruising from Kalimpong to Darjeeling with my brother and cousin. The hills, the turns, and the banter in the car kept the mood light, almost mundane. Until my phone buzzed. It was a message from my wife, Yudenla. I casually opened it, expecting something routine—perhaps a reminder or a meme. What I saw instead made my heart skip a beat.

A photo. Two faint lines on a pregnancy test stick.

Time seemed to freeze. My hands trembled slightly, my breathing caught mid-thought. I stared at the image, and a wave of emotions flooded through me. Happiness, disbelief, confusion, anxiety, and above all—an overwhelming sense of responsibility. In that split second, I knew my life had changed. I was going to be a father.

Yet, I couldn't shout with joy or shed tears of excitement. Not yet. In our culture, it's customary to keep such news private during the first trimester. It's a mix of tradition, spirituality, and fear—an old belief that keeping the pregnancy a secret guards it from bad luck or evil eyes. But that cultural norm collided with the reality that my cousin had already peeked over my shoulder and seen the message. The secret was leaking faster than I could process it.

Moments later, my phone rang. It was Yudenla. Her voice was trembling, filled with emotion. She wasn't crying, but I could sense she was on the edge. "I think I'm pregnant," she whispered. I wanted to jump out of the car, scream with joy, hug her through the phone. But instead, I swallowed all of that and simply said, "We'll talk when I get home. I'm here for you."

That night, I lay in bed replaying everything. We had been trying for a baby. We'd talked about it for months, read articles, downloaded ovulation apps, and checked calendars. Yet nothing prepares you for the actual moment when it happens. It felt surreal. It felt like winning the lottery and realizing you now need to manage a fortune.

Our journey had officially begun.

For the first few days, we kept it between us. There were tears of joy, secret smiles exchanged across the room, and an invisible bond that tightened with every hour. I started to notice every little detail about her—was she more tired than usual? Was she eating enough? Was she feeling anxious?

But along with the joy came a gnawing fear. What if something went wrong? What if the test was a false positive? What if... what if... what if? These questions don't get answered in a day. And no one tells men how to deal with them. As a husband, I didn't want to be overbearing, but I wanted to be involved. I didn't want to seem too worried, but I was.

There's no manual handed to you when your wife gets pregnant. No one prepares you for the storm of feelings, the flood of questions, or the shifts in your relationship. I remember the first time she had a food aversion—something she used to love suddenly made her nauseous. Or the day she cried while watching an old cartoon. These might sound like little things, but they were massive indicators that things were changing. Drastically.

And I had to change with them.

I had to be more patient, more observant, more helpful. I began doing more around the house, cooking occasionally, making sure she had water nearby, researching pregnancy-safe foods. We scheduled our first doctor's appointment. I accompanied her, holding her hand as we stepped into this new world of prenatal scans, folic acid tablets, and weekly development charts.

Emotionally, I was a wreck—but a silent one. I didn't tell anyone what I was feeling. Men are taught to be strong, to not cry, to not show vulnerability. But let me tell you, when I saw that first scan, the little blinking heart on the monitor, I nearly lost it. That heartbeat—it was my child. A life I had helped create. I felt pride, fear, hope, and love all colliding inside me. And I had no roadmap for any of it.

At night, we would talk for hours. She would ask me if I was ready, if I was scared. I would tell her the truth—I was scared, but I was also committed. I knew this would be the most important journey of our lives. I promised her I would walk every step with her.

We debated names. We imagined what the baby would look like. We started noting down lists of things we'd need. And yet, in the back of our minds, we still knew we were in the early days. Anything could happen. The joy was tempered by caution.

Then came the sharing of the news. First to our immediate family, carefully choosing words and watching expressions. My siblings were stunned. "You? A dad?" they laughed. And I laughed too, but deep down I knew—I was growing into this role faster than I ever imagined.

In this chapter, I want other men to know—it's okay to feel overwhelmed. It's okay to be scared. It's okay to not know what to say. But don't shut down. Don't ignore what's happening. Engage, ask questions, be there—even if you don't have the answers.

Being a father starts long before the baby arrives. It begins the moment you see those two lines. From that point on, your thoughts, your priorities, your heart—they all start shifting. Embrace that shift.

Talk to your wife. Tell her how you feel. Celebrate the little milestones together. Be vulnerable. Be strong, yes—but let strength include sensitivity.

Because this journey isn't just about bringing a baby into the world. It's about becoming a better partner, a better man, and eventually—a great father.

And that, my brothers, starts from the very first message.

CHAPTER II

The First Trimester – Fear in the Fog

They say the first three months are the most delicate—not just for the baby, but for the parents too. Especially for first timers like us, walking into the unknown with shaky feet and a thousand questions. Looking back now, those early weeks felt like walking through a fog. You can see only a few steps ahead, and every sound, every twitch, every pause makes you stop and wonder—*Is everything okay?*

Physically, Yudenla was beginning to feel it. Fatigue hit her hard. She would nap twice a day and still go to bed early. Smells that never bothered her suddenly became unbearable—garlic, boiled eggs, even the scent of her favourite shampoo. Her relationship with food turned unpredictable. One moment she was craving spicy instant noodles; the next, she couldn't even look at them without gagging.

Emotionally, she was on a roller coaster. And I was buckled into the seat right beside her.

One evening, around the 7th week, I found her crying softly in the kitchen. She wasn't in pain. Nothing had happened. But she felt overwhelmed, anxious, and strangely guilty. "I don't feel like myself," she whispered. I didn't have a solution. I just held her, trying to pour every ounce of reassurance into that hug. That's when I began to understand—support isn't always about fixing things. Sometimes, it's just about being there.

I remember the day of our first ultrasound. It was both terrifying and magical. The room was cold, and the screen in front of us flickered with static before revealing a tiny blob—our baby. And then we saw it: the flicker of a heartbeat. Fast. Steady. Alive. That tiny flutter reassured us in a way words never could. I looked at Yudenla and saw the tears in her eyes. We were really doing this.

The doctor, calm and kind, walked us through the basics—no heavy lifting, eat small meals, take your supplements. But for me, the weight wasn't physical. It was mental. How do I keep her safe? How do I keep *them* safe? I started obsessing over checklists: prenatal vitamins, clean food, safe sleep, stress reduction, appointment dates. I began researching way too much, diving into forums, videos, and articles. A word of caution: Google is both your best friend and worst enemy during this time.

Our evenings turned quieter. We watched less TV and talked more. She would place her hand on her belly unconsciously, as if already protecting the life inside her. I found myself doing the same. Her changes became our changes. Her needs became my priority.

But not every day was tender and poetic. There were days of frustration. Days when we argued over silly things—what to eat, what to watch, when to sleep. Pregnancy hormones are real. But so is the exhaustion of the man trying to keep everything together without showing he's scared too. I had to learn to give her space, to not take things personally, and to let go of control.

We also started journaling. Not every day, but enough to mark the emotional milestones. I would write things like, "She smiled more today," or "She finally ate something she liked." Small wins that meant the world.

By the end of the first trimester, we had told our parents, shared a few whispers with close friends, and began imagining our future with a little more clarity. The fog wasn't completely gone, but the light was beginning to break through.

If there's onc thing I want every man to remember from this chapter, it's this: your presence matters more than your perfection. You don't have to be a doctor, a therapist, or a hero. Just be there. Hold her hand. Laugh when you can. Cry when you must. But don't walk behind or ahead. Walk beside her.

Because in that first trimester, you're not just nurturing a child—you're nurturing your relationship, your trust, and the foundation of the family you're building.

CHAPTER III

Shifting Gears – Lifestyle Changes and Reality Checks

The day the pregnancy test showed two lines, I thought the biggest change had already happened. Little did I know, that was just the spark. The real changes began after the first doctor's visit, the first sonogram, and the first time I saw my wife turn down coffee because "the smell made her sick."

Let's talk about *lifestyle changes*—and I don't just mean hers. I mean yours too.

Pregnancy doesn't just happen to your partner—it happens to both of you. It creeps into every corner of your daily routine, your weekend plans, your meals, your habits, and even your sleep. And as a man, you have to rewire your life *with intention*.

First came the food. Out went the spicy street food, late-night Maggi, and undercooked meats. In came boiled veggies, fruits I couldn't name, pregnancy-safe snacks, and meals on a tight schedule. I had to learn to cook a few things—not because she couldn't, but because she *shouldn't always have to*. And honestly? I became pretty good at it.

We began tracking her meals, making sure she had enough iron, calcium, and folic acid. I'd read labels in grocery stores, cross-check ingredients, and even argue with pharmacists about which supplements were best. It wasn't glamorous, but it was necessary.

Then came the sleep schedule. Or should I say, the *lack* of one? She'd wake up at 2 AM hungry, or needing to pee, or because her legs were cramping. And I'd be right there—half asleep—helping her to the bathroom, rubbing her back, or just sitting with her while she ate dry toast in the dark.

You don't realize how precious uninterrupted sleep is until it's gone.

Social life? That changed too. Our outings got shorter. No more crowded restaurants or long road trips. She got tired quickly. And as her partner, I had to adjust. That meant canceling plans, choosing quieter spots, and sometimes just staying home with a good movie and her feet in my lap.

Was it hard? Yes.

Did I miss my old routines? Definitely.

But every time I saw her belly grow, every time she placed my hand on it to feel a tiny kick, I was reminded of why it was worth it.

Emotionally, I also had to mature. You see, before pregnancy, your world is largely about *you*. Your work, your friends, your plans. But when a baby's on the way, your focus needs to shift. Not out of guilt, but out of love and responsibility. It's about asking: "What can I do to make this easier for her? Safer for the baby? Better for our family?"

That's when you start letting go of ego and convenience.

I also cut back on drinking. Not because she asked—but because it felt wrong to be intoxicated while she had to stay clean and cautious every single day. Solidarity, even in small things, matters.

We also began organizing finances. Hospital bills, scans, vitamins, baby gear—it all adds up fast. We made spreadsheets, started a baby fund, and reviewed our insurance. Suddenly, I wasn't just a husband—I was becoming a planner, protector, and provider in a deeper way.

Was it overwhelming? At times, yes.

But that's what this phase is about—*becoming*. Growing into the role before the baby ever arrives.

If you're reading this and you're feeling nervous, know that's a good sign. It means you care. Just remember: you don't have to be perfect. You just have to be *present*—in the discomfort, in the changes, in the day-to-day reality.

Because pregnancy doesn't just create a child.

It creates a father.

CHAPTER IV

Cravings, Comfort, and Confusion

The second trimester began with a gentle shift—a ray of sunshine after weeks of fog. The morning sickness started to fade. The fatigue didn't feel so heavy. There was even laughter again, that lightness in her eyes that I had missed. But with that return of energy came something new: cravings. And let me tell you, cravings are no joke.

For most men, cravings seem like a cute phase—your wife wants pickles, or ice cream, or something spicy. But for me, it turned into a full-time mission. One night, she desperately wanted a specific Bengali mishti (sweet). Not just any mishti—the kind with a creamy saffron top and soaked in syrup, from a particular shop that closed in 40 minutes. I ran like a man possessed. Got it. Came back breathless. She smiled, took a bite, then paused. "Hmm... I think I want chocolate instead."

At first, I felt frustrated. I had just sprinted across town, dodging traffic and vendors. But when I looked at her—holding the mishti with a shy, sheepish smile—I realized this wasn't about the sweet. It was about comfort. Hormones were making her body crave things her brain couldn't even process. Her desires weren't rooted in logic, but in feeling. And as a partner, I had to lean into that, not question it.

There was also the emotional turbulence. Some days she'd wake up smiling, humming tunes, radiant with joy. Other days, she'd curl up in bed, overwhelmed by anxiety, unsure of her body, her future, and everything in between. The second trimester is often called the "honeymoon phase" of pregnancy, but it's also a period of intense emotional processing.

One evening, we were sitting quietly after dinner. She turned to me and asked, "Will I still be beautiful after I get big?" I was stunned. To me, she was glowing—carrying our child, strong and brave. But to her, the changes in her body were scary. She was worried about stretch marks, about not fitting into her favorite clothes, about losing her identity.

I held her hand and said something I had been meaning to for days: "You're more beautiful now than ever. Because I see you becoming a mother. And that is a kind of beauty the world doesn't talk about enough."

We didn't solve everything in that conversation. But she smiled. And sometimes, that's enough.

We started preparing for the baby's arrival—slowly. Browsing cribs online, discussing nursery colors, thinking about diapers, breast pumps, and strollers. And through all of this, I learned that part of my role was to bring calm to the chaos. When her hormones made everything feel urgent, I had to be the gentle reminder that it was okay to take it one step at a time.

To the men reading this: your job isn't just to fetch sweets or rub her feet. Your job is to *see* her. To make her feel safe, cherished, and supported. Cravings and confusion will come and go—but how you respond to them will stay in her memory forever.

This is the time to become her partner in the deepest sense—not just in the fun baby name debates, but in the quiet reassurances, the late-night talks, and the constant showing up.

This chapter is about realizing that love, in pregnancy, looks a lot like service. And in serving, you grow.

CHAPTER V

When a Boy Becomes a Father

There comes a moment in every man's journey to fatherhood when something changes—not around him, but within. It's a slow-burning realization, not announced by fireworks or ceremonies. It creeps in during the quietest of moments. Maybe while watching your wife sleep, hand gently resting on her belly. Maybe while folding tiny baby clothes. Or maybe when you look in the mirror and no longer recognize the man staring back at you—not because you've lost yourself, but because you've become someone new.

That moment hit me somewhere in the middle of the second trimester.

By then, the pregnancy was no longer a secret. Our close family knew. A few friends did too. We had begun sharing small updates—doctor visits, heartbeat recordings, funny cravings, mood swings. It was starting to feel real. Tangible. Heavy, in the best and worst ways.

But it wasn't just Yudenla who was changing.

I was changing too.

I remember the evening I stood in the bathroom, brushing my teeth, staring blankly at my reflection. My thoughts weren't on the workday I'd had or the plans for the weekend. They were swirling around baby names, college funds, insurance policies, and prenatal yoga. I was 13 years deep into adulthood, but in that moment, I truly felt the weight of *becoming a father*.

The transition from being a "man" to a "dad" isn't sudden. It's not when the baby arrives. It starts months earlier, in the way you think, act, and feel. The carefree part of you begins to fade, replaced by a version who calculates every decision twice. You start saving more, worrying more, caring more.

I began noticing risks I had never noticed before—slippery stairs, sharp corners, news headlines about unsafe baby products. I started Googling things I had once made fun of—"best air purifiers for newborns," "is ghee safe during pregnancy," "how to change a diaper without crying." My YouTube algorithm turned into a dad-baby workshop, and I didn't even mind.

Emotionally, I started to shift from being a husband who supports, to a father who protects. This wasn't about macho bravado. This was about a deeply primal instinct that kicked in unexpectedly. I wanted to shield

Yudenla from every emotional hiccup, every ounce of pain, every moment of doubt. I couldn't always do that, but I *wanted* to. That intention itself changed me.

I also became more introspective. I thought about my own childhood. My relationship with my father. The things I wished he had done differently. The things he did right. The memories that stuck. I realized that I wasn't just about to become someone's father—I was about to become someone's entire *world*. Every decision I made would shape her life. Every word I spoke could become a core memory. Every failure, every success, every hug, every fight—they would all be absorbed by this tiny human being like sponge on water.

And then I thought about *my wife*—this incredible woman who was carrying our child, day and night, with courage and grace.

She was going through changes that I could never fully understand. Her body was stretching, reshaping, aching. Her emotions were riding a never-ending rollercoaster. And yet, there were moments she still worried *about me*—whether I was sleeping well, eating right, managing stress. That selflessness amazed me.

One night, after a quiet dinner, she sat beside me and said, "I hope I don't change too much after the baby. I still want us." That sentence cracked something open inside me.

Because in that moment, I realized: as much as we were preparing for a baby, we also had to prepare for *us*. Our bond. Our marriage. Our friendship. The baby wasn't just entering a family. The baby was entering a relationship. And that relationship needed to be strong.

So, I started doing something I hadn't done enough of—*checking in with her*. Not just "are you okay?" but deeper questions. "What are you scared of right now?" "What do you miss the most?" "What can I do today to make you feel loved?"

These questions opened doors. She began to share things she was keeping in, even from herself. Fears of childbirth. Fear of being alone. Fear of losing her identity. Fear that I might not find her attractive post-pregnancy.

And I reassured her—not just with words, but with actions. With back rubs when she didn't ask. With handwritten notes on the bathroom mirror. With small treats that made her smile. With uninterrupted attention during our walks, where we talked about the kind of parents we wanted to be.

I was learning to be present—not just physically, but emotionally.

I also had to face my own shadows. There were days I was frustrated—at her moods, at my own helplessness, at the sheer unknown of everything. There were moments I snapped, then immediately felt guilty. But I began to understand: frustration doesn't make you a bad husband. It makes you human. What matters is how you handle it. I started journaling. Meditating. Giving myself grace while striving to do better.

Some nights, I would lie awake and talk to the baby in her belly. "Hey little one," I'd whisper. "It's your dad. I'm right here. We're waiting for you." Those moments became sacred. They weren't for Instagram stories or baby books. They were just for us—for me, to begin the bond early. And perhaps for her, to know that her father's voice was soft, kind, and constant.

To the men reading this, let me say this loud and clear: it's okay to grieve your old self. It's okay to feel like you're losing the carefree version of who you were. But don't fight the change. Lean into it.

Because what you're becoming is something bigger. You are becoming *home* for someone. Their first protector. Their first storyteller. Their first hero.

This chapter of pregnancy may not come with belly kicks or hormonal cravings. But it will mark the internal journey of manhood—where a boy steps back, and a father steps forward.

The transition isn't easy. It's not glamorous. But it's real. And it's the most important work you'll ever do.

CHAPTER VI

Third Trimester – The Wait, the Weight, and the What-Ifs

The third trimester came in quietly—no fireworks, no big announcement. Just a deeper belly, a louder heartbeat at every scan, and the steady approach of D-Day. What started as a dot on a test stick was now a kicking, twisting, hiccupping little person inside my wife. And with each passing week, the reality became heavier—not just for her, but for me too.

We were on the final stretch, and everything felt... intense.

Around the beginning of the third trimester, something unexpected happened. A routine blood test showed that Yudenla's platelet count was dropping. She didn't have any visible symptoms—no bruising, no fatigue—but our doctor wasn't willing to take a chance. She referred us to one of the best haematologists in Bangalore. And that's when the anxiety began to creep in.

We had several visits with the haematologist. He didn't sound too alarmed. "Let's just observe for now," he said. Logical, yes. But emotionally, those words didn't settle anything. I found myself googling platelet counts late into the night, cross-referencing numbers, reading about worst-case scenarios I had no business reading.

Still, we moved forward. We held on.

By the time we hit the 38th week, the haematologist decided it was time to intervene. He prescribed a five-day course of steroids, hoping it would boost her platelet levels enough to make delivery safer. Those five days felt like a tightrope walk. Each night, I watched her sleep and wondered what was going on inside her body—inside her womb, inside her blood.

And then came April 28th.

We got the new platelet count—and it had gone up. Relief washed over me like cold water after a long run. I remember updating our gynecologist immediately, not knowing what to expect next. She listened carefully, then said the words that threw me off balance:

"Let's do the C-section tomorrow."

Tomorrow?

I was outside when I got the call. I felt stunned. Not in fear, not in joy—just sheer *shock*. I called Yudenla right away. There was no panic in her voice. Just this calm resolve.

She said, "Let's do it."

And just like that, it was time.

We got admitted to the hospital that same night at 9 PM. No dramatic water breaking. No frantic ambulance. Just a quiet ride, packed bags, nervous hands, and a baby who was about to meet the world.

The hospital was cold and bright and sterile, but our emotions were warm, loud, and all over the place. I tried to be composed for her, but inside, I was pacing in every direction. The next morning, April 29th, we were scheduled for the surgery at 10 AM.

Yudenla was taken into the OT first. I stood outside, trying to breathe slow. Fifteen minutes passed.

Then a nurse came out and called me in.

My heart dropped. My mind spun. *Why are they calling me in? Is something wrong?*

I walked into that OT with a stomach full of knots.

But there were no complications. No emergencies. Just my wife, prepped and covered, and a team ready to bring our baby into the world. I stood beside her head, holding her hand, whispering every bit of strength I had left in me.

And then we heard it.

That first cry.

Time paused.

We took a deep breath—together. I looked at her eyes, misty and tired, and she looked at mine. That moment... that exact second... was the most *real* I've ever felt in my entire life.

Our baby was here. And nothing else mattered.

You know, as a man, you don't get to feel the kicks inside you. You don't deal with the swelling or the sleepless nights or the hormonal rollercoasters. But when you're standing there, holding your wife's hand during her C-section, watching her give everything she has—your job is clear.

You show up.

You be her anchor.

You stay strong even if you're breaking inside.

You be the person she can rely on without even asking.

That's not about being macho. It's about being *present*. About being a *partner*.

After all the what-ifs, the hospital visits, the falling platelets, the steroid treatments, and the months of waiting—the moment had finally come. And we walked through it not just as a couple, but as a *team*.

To all the men reading this: trust your instincts when the moment comes. You'll be scared. You'll be clueless. But you'll also be exactly who she needs—*as long as you show up.*

Because when your child enters this world crying, you'll know something deeper than words:

This... is what everything was for.

CHAPTER VII

The Delivery Room – A Storm of Emotions

You think the hard part is over once the baby is out. You think the weight lifts. That now it's just lullabies, diapers, and smiling selfies with your newborn.

But nothing prepares you for the emotional storm that hits right after birth.

When we heard her cry for the first time, I felt something shift deep in my chest. It wasn't just love. It was something *bigger* — something primal, ancient, beyond logic. Like I was meeting a piece of myself I didn't know was missing.

They wrapped her quickly and brought her near us.

She was so tiny. So unbelievably delicate.

Her face was crumpled. Her fingers, curled. And her voice — oh, that cry — it echoed through me like a calling. I reached out and touched her soft cheek, and that was it.

I was gone.

No one teaches you how to feel in that moment. You don't know whether to laugh or cry. I did both. So did Yudenla. And we didn't care who saw.

The team was still stitching her up. She was exhausted, but she kept asking about the baby, "Is she okay? Did she cry? Is she healthy?"

I kept saying yes.

Yes.

Yes.

Even if my voice was cracking.

We were taken to the recovery room next, and I held our daughter in my arms for the very first time. She was calm, resting on my chest, wrapped like a little bundle of stardust. In that moment, I wasn't a husband or a soon-to-be father. I was a **protector**. A **provider**. A **witness** to a miracle.

Yudenla was wheeled in soon after, groggy but smiling. That tired smile — God, I'll never forget it. The kind of smile that says: *We did it. We made it.*

That first night was a blur.

Visitors came. Nurses checked. Forms were signed. But all I remember is the three of us, together. A new family. A new world.

We hadn't even picked her name fully yet. But names didn't matter that night.

She was *ours*.

And I'll be honest — I didn't sleep.

Not because the baby was crying. Not because I was tired.

But because I couldn't stop staring.

I watched her chest rise and fall. I watched my wife sleep beside us, bruised but beautiful. And I kept whispering, "Thank you. Thank you. Thank you."

In those first few hours, you realize how little you know about being a parent — and how much you're willing to learn.

You become someone new, not all at once, but breath by breath.

And if I can offer one piece of advice for other men: *Don't run from the emotions.* Feel them. Let them crash over you. Cry if you need to. Smile if you can. But stay present.

Because these are the minutes that become stories. These are the hours that change you.

And when you look back years later, it won't be the hospital lights or the paperwork or the panic you'll remember.

It'll be that cry.

That touch.

That first time you whispered her name and felt the universe shift.

From Man To Father – The Greatest Evolution

There was a time I believed strength was in silence — in enduring quietly, providing without emotion, and standing like a rock no matter the storm. But pregnancy shattered that illusion. It taught me that true strength lies in softness, in patience, in presence.

As I now hold Prayushi in my arms and look at Yudenla resting beside me, I realize something profound: I didn't just witness a birth — I was reborn too.

This journey began with confusion, anxiety, and the pressure of being "the man" in the relationship. But it ended with clarity, purpose, and a kind of love I never imagined possible. I learned that supporting your wife isn't just about lifting bags or fetching cravings. It's about being emotionally available. It's about understanding the moments she herself doesn't understand. It's about whispering, "You're beautiful," when she feels like a stranger in her own body. It's about rubbing her back not because she asks, but because you see her eyes sink from exhaustion.

It's about apologizing when you fall short. About holding her when she cries, even if you don't know why she's crying. And more importantly — never using her hormonal state as an excuse to be careless with your words.

This book was born out of honesty. I wanted every man — the quiet one, the scared one, the overconfident one — to know that it's okay to not have all the answers. What matters is that you show up, again and again, with your heart open.

To the man reading this: You are not just a spectator in this journey. You are her teammate, her anchor, and your child's first superhero.

From the moment those two lines appear on a test to the first cry echoing through the delivery room, you will be tested in ways no book or YouTube video can fully prepare you for. But if you lean in — not run — you'll come out the other side as someone new. A man forged in love, resilience, and humility.

I stepped into this journey as Praneev — a husband learning the ropes.

I walked out as a father.

And that... is the greatest title I'll ever carry.

What Every Man Must Learn On The Journey To Fatherhood

1. Hormones Are Real — Respect Them

Before pregnancy, I had heard jokes about "pregnancy mood swings." But I didn't understand how real they are until I lived with them. It's not just someone being "extra emotional" — her entire body chemistry is changing.

What I learned:

- Don't argue logic in the middle of a meltdown.
- Don't say "you're overreacting."
- Instead, say:

  - "It's okay, I'm here."
  - "Do you want to talk about it or just need a hug?"
  - "You're doing so well, even on tough days."

Sometimes, silence and presence are more comforting than trying to "fix" things.

2. Mood Swings Aren't Personal

She may be angry, distant, or overly affectionate all in one day. It's not because of *you*. It's because her body is navigating a hormonal tsunami.

What I learned:

- Stay consistent. Be her anchor.
- Let her vent. You don't need to reply to every complaint.
- If she lashes out, don't respond with ego. Respond with empathy.
- Sometimes she just wants to feel heard, not helped.

3. Be Actively Present, Not Just Physically Around

Presence isn't just about being in the room. It's about noticing:

- Her feet swelling.
- Her changing relationship with food.
- The way she silently stares out the window longer than usual.

What I learned:

- Offer water before she asks.
- Rub her back while she's lying down.
- Say "I'm proud of you" — often. Not just when she's glowing but especially when she's exhausted.

4. Understand Her Fears — Don't Downplay Them

Even if everything medically is okay, pregnancy brings irrational fears.

- "What if I'm not a good mom?"
- "What if something happens to the baby?"
- "What if my body never feels the same?"

What I learned:

- Never say "don't worry" and leave it at that.
- Instead, say:

  - "Whatever happens, we're in this together."
  - "You don't have to go through this alone."
  - "You're already an amazing mother — I see it every day."

5. Stay Curious and Keep Learning

Don't wait for her to tell you what a folic acid tablet is or what her blood test means. Ask. Research. Be part of it.

What I learned:

- Ask the doctor questions. Take notes.
- Join pregnancy groups online. Listen to podcasts.
- Understand platelet counts, gestational diabetes, early signs of labor — not because you're the doctor, but because you're the *partner*.

6. Be Her Advocate in the Medical System

Doctors are busy. Nurses rotate. It's easy for concerns to be brushed off. Your job is to ask follow-up questions, push when needed, and document everything.

What I learned:

- Ask: "What are the side effects of this medicine?"

- Confirm: "Should we get a second opinion?"
- Be polite, but assertive.

7. Build a Routine of Reassurance

Pregnancy often makes women feel unattractive, insecure, and uncertain.

What I did:

- Complimented her daily, even when she didn't feel like herself.
- Reminded her that she was doing the most important job on earth.
- Took photos with her — not just to post, but to preserve the journey.

8. Prepare for the Unexpected — And Adapt Quickly

We didn't expect platelet complications. We didn't expect a sudden C-section call. But parenthood starts with accepting that *control* is an illusion.

What I learned:

- Always keep your hospital bag ready.
- Trust your doctor, but also *trust your gut*.
- In chaos, you must become calm — not perfect, but *calm*.

9. Make Memories, Not Just Plans

We spent months planning. But our best memories? Laughing during her mood swings, night walks, spontaneous talks about baby names, her craving for specific sweets.

What I learned:

- Don't just countdown weeks. *Live them.*
- Take videos, voice notes, write journal entries.
- Someday, your child will love knowing how they came into the world.

The Journey Ahead

As I held our daughter for the first time, I realized this was the end of one journey — and the start of a far greater one.

Fatherhood is no longer just an idea. It's a living, breathing little human who will look up to me. But I now understand — it's not enough to "be a dad." You have to **be the kind of man** your child would admire. And that begins long before birth.

So to every man reading this — here's the truth:

- You're not just a support system. You are *part* of the pregnancy.
- You don't need to have all the answers. But you do need to show up, consistently and kindly.
- This isn't about being perfect. It's about being *present* — in every craving, every cry, every heartbeat.

This is the end of *Part One*. But the manual doesn't stop here.

Because after the delivery, the real test begins — raising a child, protecting your marriage, balancing dreams with diapers, and learning who you are all over again.

And so — I'll see you in **Part Two: A Man's Manual – Fatherhood Begins**.

With love,